LIGHTHOUSES
of Michigan

tanding on a sand dune, waiting for the sunset at the North Pier in St. Joseph, I could not help noticing at least two hundred gulls flying around the harbor entrance. There was no particular pattern and they were not feeding. Not one dropped to the water to pick anything up. It looked like they were flying for the joy of it and simply cruising around the harbor on a pleasant summer evening. It reminded me of the 1950's when it was popular for young people to jump in a car and cruise around town just for fun.

My mind drifted back to that time when fishing with a cane pole in the harbor at the St. Joseph - Benton Harbor waterfront was a popular activity. In the shadow of the North Pier Lighthouse, fishermen would vie for the best positions, dipping bait minnows from the river on one side of the pier and using them to catch perch on the other. On weekends, especially, there would be a flurry of activity as fishermen and spectators joined in laughter and camaraderie.

I had moved to southwest Michigan in 1950 to further my education and soon the lighthouse at St. Joseph became an old friend. To stand beside it was a tremendous thrill! Close-up it was big, bold and rugged, but when you viewed it from the shore at sunset it produced a certain delicate aura of romance. The sound of voices would be hushed as couples, strolling hand in hand, were captured by its spell. It was such a delightful way to watch the dimming of the day. Two years later I acquired my first camera and photography became a passion. My love for nature and the out-of-doors has influenced my photography ever since.

1. - North Pier Lighthouse on a warm summer morning from the bluff in St. Joseph, 2. - South Haven on a windy day, 3. - Gulls in flight, twilight at St. Joseph's Tiscornia Park, 4. - Sunset at South Haven, 5. - "Big Red", Holland Harbor Light as viewed from Holland State Park.

1

4

5

Grand Haven

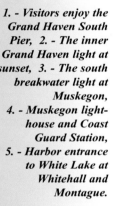

1. - Visitors enjoy the Grand Haven South Pier, 2. - The inner Grand Haven light at sunset, 3. - The south breakwater light at Muskegon, 4. - Muskegon lighthouse and Coast Guard Station, 5. - Harbor entrance to White Lake at Whitehall and Montague.

6

2

1

3

5

With the purchase of my first boat, the lighthouse took on an entirely new dimension. With only a compass and depth finder for instrumentation, I dared to venture offshore and even out of sight of land! Next came the first excursion to a new port. On a sunny spring day, South Haven was my destination, some 30 miles north. Nearing South Haven, the warming air next to the cold water of Lake Michigan suddenly enclosed me in a dense fog. Being an inexperienced boater, finding the harbor in heavy fog presented a real challenge. Stopping the boat and shutting off the engine I listened intently for the fog signal, then headed in the direction of the sound. Repeating this several times brought me right up to the bright red lighthouse at South Haven. Once in port, I had lunch, then headed back to St. Joseph. Just as quickly as the fog had descended, it lifted. The return trip was clear and smooth.

But now, I must deal with the sea gulls still milling around. The ideal exposure would be with a slow shutter speed to smooth the waves, however it would make the gulls unrecognizable. After several variations, I decided to try an old trick. On the last picture on the roll of film, I left the shutter open for 30 seconds to allow the birds to fly through without being seen. The resulting picture on page one has been used on post cards, calendars and tee shirts.

4

7

1

Another boat and another time found me exploring the West Michigan coastline with my youngest son Mike, age 10, and our Weimaraner dog named Blue. Doing post card pictures, we had traveled as far as Leland, visiting every port along the way. The weather was fair and delightful. Little did we know what lie in store for us. Heading back down the lake, we passed the Little Sable Point Lighthouse at Silver Lake at about 5:00 P.M. intending to get to Montague and White Lake for the evening. Rounding the point, we faced into the wind and a nasty, choppy sea that slowed our progress to a crawl. As the wind increased, common sense and a survival instinct strongly suggested that we turn around and seek shelter in the nearest port, which was Pentwater. Every boater on the lake must have had the same idea, except they got there first. Not a single boat slip in the entire harbor was available. As night came, we found a tiny canal and sensing the impending storm, we double tied the boat and put on life vests. Even our pet dog got a life vest! With a small portable TV, we watched the weather radar broadcast tornado warnings as the storm swept over us. The wind raged and the lightning was incredible. Two boats sank in the Pentwater harbor that night from lightning strikes that perforated their fiberglass hulls.

Three days later at 5:00 A.M., we ventured out on the lake and headed south toward St. Joseph. A following sea with four foot waves was not too bad and passing the Little Sable Point Lighthouse again we ran close to shore and stayed in somewhat sheltered water almost to Grand Haven where we went ashore for a meal and to get fuel. The north wind was steadily increasing and on Lake Michigan, whitecaps were blowing off of every cresting wave. Turning south and running with the wind, I headed toward Holland. The waves seemed larger near land, so we went further out to sea. By the time we passed the harbor at Holland, we were five miles off shore. We tried to run the same speed as the waves, but the water was far too rough to allow that. It was

2

4

1. - White River Light Station, Montague, 2. - Little Sable Point from Lake Michigan, 3. - Evening at the beach with Little Sable Point Light, 4. - Inside a Third Order Fresnel Lens, 5. - This 1970 photograph of Little Sable Point shows the tower when it was painted white.

5

impossible to run back to Holland, so there was no choice except to continue. The larger the waves became the smaller our boat seemed. Wild waves were overtaking us from behind and it was most uncomfortable, to put it mildly. One moment we would be on top of the world and could see forever. But there in front of us would be a hole in the lake, large enough to put a house in! The next moment, we were in that hole with a wall of water on every side. The waves reached a height of fifteen to eighteen feet and our boat was only eighteen feet long and not very tall! In reality we were making fairly good progress, but struggling with every wave, it seemed to take forever.

At St. Joseph, the waves were washing right over both

3

Little Sable Point

breakwaters making it very difficult to even enter the harbor. Once inside the harbor, people were standing along the side waving to us, boats were everywhere and there was even a band playing at the end of State Street. What a wonderful way to celebrate our homecoming! It was then that we realized we had inadvertently landed right in the middle of St. Joseph's Venetian Festival. We tied up to a sea wall near the courthouse to find a telephone and call home. Our dog, Blue, was more interested in finding a tree. Calling home we were told our arrival had been broadcast on television. The camera had zoomed in on us and they recognized the lone boat that came in from the lake.

1. - Harbor entrance at Pentwater,
2. - Pentwater sunset from Mears State Park, 3. - Sailboats at rest on a summer morning at Pentwater.

1

2

3

There are few sporting activities that cause people to question one's sanity more than fishing! The introduction of salmon in Lake Michigan instantly made Manistee a famous fishing "hot spot." Thousands of fishermen descended on the community. While doing photos, just getting around in traffic was a problem, but there were plenty of things on the "light side" which made it all worthwhile. There was a scene along the Manistee River where people stood shoulder to shoulder on both sides, casting into the river. Watching from a bridge, I saw a man give a tremendous yank and shouted, "fish on!" Another fisherman across the river also shouted, "fish on!" and started tugging. Each one, in turn, was nearly pulled into the water before realizing they had each other's lines!

There was another incident when a fisherman was standing in the river with waders on. Unfortunately, he was in water that came four inches above his waders. It was a good thing there were enough people beside him to keep him from being pulled over!

A pharmacist told me of a doctor friend of his who was treating a lady in the emergency room with a fishhook in her ear. Voicing his real concern over the matter, her husband said to the doctor, "Whatever you have to do, please don't ruin my lure!"

14

4

Many times I joined the parade of boats that would gather in the pre-dawn darkness and motor out the Manistee channel, en masse, passing the lighthouse and entering Lake Michigan. No one talked much. We knew where we were. Secretly, I think the big question was "why would we be out here milling around in the dark at this time of the night?" But when you connected with one of those powerful king salmon whose first run would make your reel scream, it would bring such a rush of excitement that you just had to return again and again. I was hooked on the sport!

5

6

7

8

1. - Ludington North Pier Light,
2. - Ludington North Pier Light as viewed from the Badger, car ferry boat,
3. - Big Sable Point Lighthouse north of Ludington State Park,
4. - Big Sable Point Lighthouse, open for tours during the summer months,
5. - Manistee North Pierhead Light,
6. - Author with a prize Chinook Salmon at Manistee,
7. - Fishing activity at Manistee,
8. - Fishermen on the North Pier at sunset, Manistee.

15

Point Betsie Lighthouse

1

2

In the summer of 1983, I made a two week boat trip into northern Lake Michigan at a time that would coincide with the annual Chicago to Mackinac sailboat race. Fifteen year old Rich Balenci, a friend of the family, went along with me, partly for the adventure but also to visit his sister who had a summer job at Alford Drug Store on Mackinac Island. With 10-speed bikes, sleeping bags, camp stove, coolers and cameras aboard we were quite the explorers. The weather was excellent as we visited each coastal town doing photography. The bicycles gave us a good range and the 26-foot Starcraft boat became our home.

Loran-C navigation equipment allowed us to plot a very accurate course and travel in fog or darkness. The equipment would tell us how far to our destination, what course to steer, present speed and estimated time of arrival. It allowed us to travel in the fog from the Frankfort harbor to South Manitou Island, making two course changes in the Manitou Passage. We came right up to the lighthouse more than forty miles away without ever seeing land, or for that matter, even another boat.

Rich and I spent a day and night at South Manitou Island bicycling around the old roads and visiting the lighthouse. We

3

4

5

6

1. - *South Manitou Island Lighthouse, Sleeping Bear Dunes National Lakeshore,* 2. - *Twisted cedar tree still smells of cedar after being buried in the sand for 3,500 years on South Manitou Island,* 3. - *Francisco Morazon shipwreck lies just offshore,* 4. - *Exploring inside the engine room,* 5. - *Only rust and memories remain on deck,* 6. - *A newly hatched sea gull chick greets the world on the Francisco Morazon.*

even went inside the rusting hull of the *Francisco Morazon* ship that ran aground and was abandoned just south of the island. It makes a great nesting place for barn swallows and sea gulls.

The following day we motored on, passing under the Mackinac Bridge, arriving at Mackinac Island a few hours ahead of the racing sailboats. During the night, so many sailboats arrived in the harbor, they overflowed the space and had to raft together at the docks. It was an exciting event. In the morning, extracting ourselves required moving six sailboats.

After a couple of days at Mackinac Island, we worked our way back. En route to Beaver Island, we ran along side a thousand foot ore boat for awhile. We also visited Sleeping Bear Dunes and even took some time for fishing before returning home. Bringing back the images taken along the way is my way to share the experience with others.

19

The scenic area from Empire around the Leelanau Peninsula to Traverse City and Old Mission Peninsula is some of the most diverse and lovely parts of Michigan. There are high bluffs, sweeping beaches, lovely sand dunes, quaint villages and rolling hills with attractive orchards. I travel this area often and visit the five lighthouses located in the region. With each visit to these lighthouses, it seems there are additional picture possibilities. Sometimes things just happen to come together at the right moment, like the day I was having lunch at the high overlook at Elberta Bluff. The big telephoto lens was accidentally left attached to one of the cameras when an airborne visitor, a man on a paraglider, dropped in from the sky. No time to even focus, I got off three quick shots as he came down in line with the lighthouse. The resulting post card picture titled "Frankfort, Drop in Anytime", is very popular.

A recent twilight picture of Point Betsie was made while waiting for a possible sunset. It was mostly cloudy and the colors were never bright, but after the light came on, a number of exposures were made which captured the delicate mood of the evening.

6

7

8

1. - Sunset at Frankfort's North
Breakwater Light, 2. - An unusual photo
of the Frankfort Lighthouse from the
Elberta Bluff, 3. - Lifesaving boat,
4. - Sleeping Bear Point Coast Guard
Station at Sleeping Bear Dunes operated
from 1902 to 1944, 5. - Michigan's
newest lighthouse, the Robert H. Manning
Memorial Lighthouse, at Empire, 1991,
6. - Point Betsie at twilight, 7. - Grand
Traverse Light at Northport, 8. - Old
Mission Peninsula, Traverse City.

1

Cash, my big black Labrador Retriever, and I spent a somewhat relaxing Wednesday in Charlevoix. My intentions were to visit the lighthouses of northern Lake Michigan, but the wind made the lake too rough for comfortable travel. The following day dawned calm and clear, so leaving port shortly after daylight, we were on our way towards Beaver Island. Swells from the previous day's waves could still be seen, but the surface itself was glassy smooth. It was a comfortable ride as I set the boat on autopilot and followed a course toward the lighthouse on the south end of Beaver Island. Land was soon out of sight and we were very much alone. Somehow the lake seemed very large. In the approximate 30 mile trip, only one boat came into view. It was a sailboat making little headway because of the lack of wind. There was a slight haze and I could tell from the depth of the water and the destination on the Loran-C that we were close to the island. Proceeding slowly, land appeared, but only the tops of the trees were showing above the haze making the island look unreal as if it were floating in space. It was closer than expected. There were so many large rocks that getting ashore would be difficult if not impossible. I noticed the water rolling in places. The tip of the lighthouse was visible above the treetops, but the rugged shoreline between made it impossible to get there. Upon returning to the lake, I discovered there were huge rocks just underwater on all sides of us. We had passed between the rocks without seeing them or striking them! Somewhat shaken by the close call, I did not power up the boat to cruising speed until it was in 60 feet of water. Skirting wide to the east, Beaver Island's harbor of St. James would be the next stop.

Docking at the municipal park in St. James, I left Cash to watch the boat then bicycled all around the village doing general harbor scenes, lighthouse and museum pictures. The tall ship, *Madeline*, from Traverse City, was there on display and it was interesting to visit with the crew. From St. James Harbor, the course threaded between islands and around shoals to the Squaw Island Lighthouse and then on towards Lansing Shoal Light. Northern Lake Michigan is dotted with a large number of shoals and tiny islands. Lansing Shoal is a major light about half way between Beaver Island and Naubinway, in the Upper Peninsula.

At one time, Lansing Shoal was marked by a lightship until a permanent lighthouse was built in 1928. It sits high above the water on a large square concrete platform. Railings around the two large platforms make ideal resting places for the sea birds. I counted seventy loons perching there and there were at least as many seagulls.

Next, a course was set for White Shoal about 20 miles away. Years before, I had been there and photographed the tower but, this time

3

4

5

7

8

1. - The tall ship, Madeline, patterned after a historic schooner that sailed in northern Lake Michigan, was built in Traverse City, 2. - Beaver Island Lighthouse at St. James Harbor, 3. - Marine Museum at Beaver Island, 4. - Picturesque St. James Harbor, Beaver Island, 5. - Lansing Shoal, 6. - White Shoal, 7. - Waugoshance, 8. - Gray's Reef.

6

23

1. - Skillagalee, 2. - Charlevoix harbor entrance, 3. - Beaver Islander departing the Charlevoix harbor, 4. - U.S. Coast Guard Cutter, Acacia, based in Charlevoix, 5. - Charlevoix South Pier Light, 6. - Sunset at Charlevoix.

1

2

it had a fresh coat of paint. The spiraling red and white candy stripe design was spectacular in the afternoon sun. In the distance, thunderstorm clouds were building but it was far away and hardly noticeable. It was interesting to see the moon shining brightly in the afternoon sky. The lighthouse is massive both in size and height. The huge Second Order Fresnel has been replaced and is on display at the Great Lakes Shipwreck Museum at Whitefish Point. (See page 57) Circling around the lighthouse in water 20 feet deep, I took pictures from every angle.

Traveling on, I visited the abandoned Waugoshance Light, Gray's Reef Light and then continued on to Skillagalee or Ile Aux Galets - "Isle of Pebbles." After securing the boat at the old dock, Cash and I waded ashore. Only the white tower of the light station remains on this tiny two acre island. There were thousands of gulls here, many of which were nesting. It was so alarming to them to have visitors, especially a large black dog, that they herded all the little chicks into the water and made them swim further away for protection. On the pebble beach there were nests, if you can call them nests, consisting of two gray speckled eggs sitting on the rocks and looking very much like the rocks themselves. They were spaced about two foot apart in each direction. The seabird population was split between the Hering Gull and the Common Tern.

Cash had been trained not to chase birds, so he largely ignored them as they swooped and screamed at us. Somehow, his instinct made him careful and he never even stepped on an egg or broke one.

3

4

5

On rare occasions, you may see something that you know cannot be real. Logic does not permit it. Here, before my eyes, were wisps of black smoke coming from the tower. There was no fire, no sound, no engine running. I had noticed it at several other lighthouse towers that day. Returning to the boat, the mystery was solved. Swarms of tiny gnats, attracted to the light color had completely covered the boat making it almost black. The gnats were buzzing around the towers so thickly that they looked like smoke. Once out in the wind, a lot of the gnats were blown away, but even months later, some were found preserved between the pages of my journal.

Bidding farewell to the birds and gnats, it was time to head the craft southwest towards Charlevoix. Much lighter on fuel, but still registering enough for the 19 mile run back to port, the boat bounced a little as we headed west into the freshening wind. It was one of those rare and adventuresome days, so rewarding in many ways. I had visited 8 lighthouses, the village at St. James Harbor and had taken well over two hundred photographs. Arriving at sunset, both Cash and I were tired. But what a good tired! A day like that makes up for some that are cloudy or rainy.

6

1

2

Years ago when boaters would leave northern Lake Michigan and enter the Straits of Mackinac, there were three lights for guidance: McGulpins Point and Old Mackinac to the south, and St. Helena Island Light to the north. Since 1957, the Mackinac Bridge displays navigation lights and is a very prominent landmark both day and night. Mariners now rely on the bridge lights to travel safely through the Straits of Mackinac.

After many years of being vacant, St. Helena Island Lighthouse was in a serious condition of decay. In 1986 the Great Lakes Lighthouse Keepers Association leased the lighthouse and took on the big project of restoration of this landmark. It took many donations and thousands of hours of labor by volunteer workers, including several Boy Scout troops, to restore and save the buildings. Well known lighthouse aerial photographer, John L. Wagner, of Lansing provided the before and after photographs shown here of St. Helena Island Lighthouse.

© John L. Wagner

5

© John L. Wagner

6

1. - Old Mackinac Point Lighthouse tower, 2. - Mackinac Bridge crosses the Straits of Mackinac, 3. - Old Mackinac Point Lighthouse and bridge, 4. - Old Mackinac Point Lighthouse view from the north, 5. - St. Helena Island Light Station in dis-repair, 6. - St. Helena Island Lighthouse, restored.

30 *Seul Choix*

I t is a long stretch of Lake Michigan coastline west of the Straits of Mackinac before
any natural shelter or harbor can be reached. Seul Choix (pronounced "Sish Wa"),
named by the early French voyagers and meaning "only choice", was a natural safe
haven. In 1895 a lighthouse was built on this point and it still guides freighters into Port
Inland to load limestone. Further on, Manistique was a lumbering port and also was part
of the Ann Arbor railroad car ferry network.

While doing pictures of both Poverty Island and St. Martin Island lighthouses, Dan
Johnson and his wife Eva joined me for the one day boat trip. Dan had spent his early
years on Poverty Island where his father and grandfather were lighthouse keepers. The
family lived on the mile-long and half-mile wide island all summer, then had a residence
at Burnt Bluff on the Garden Peninsula in the winter. Dan is now living in Manistique and
working as a sales representative for Penrod/Hiawatha.

Returning to Poverty Island was a bittersweet experience for Dan. There was sadness
to see the buildings decomposing and relenting to time and elements. But on the other
hand, it was nice to come back home where so many fond memories lingered.

Dan remembers as a child that it was a great place to spend a summer. The light station, in spite of the remoteness, was more modern and up-to-date than their home on
Burnt Bluff. Propane gas was used for cooking and refrigeration. Drinking water came
directly from Lake Michigan and was pumped to a storage tank which provided water for
the kitchen and for the indoor bathrooms. An underwater cable gave them telephone service between the other area lighthouses, Washington Island and mainland Wisconsin. Each
of the three lightkeepers stationed there would receive four days a month shore leave,

1. - Poverty Island Light, 2. - St. Martin Island Light, 3. - Manistique East Breakwater Light, 4. - A tram moved supplies from the dock to the lighthouse at St. Martin Island, 5. - St. Martin keeper's residence surrounded by wild flowers.

With their coming and going, Dan's family could order supplies from the grocery store at Fairport about once a week. Supplies were unloaded at a dock next to the lighthouse, but that location was exposed to the wind and waves, so after unloading, the supply boat would dock on the opposite side of the island in a sheltered place. A well-worn foot path connected both sides of the island.

Inspectors would visit Poverty Island frequently and unannounced. Children would be "shooed" away so as not to interfere with such important business. Accurate records were kept daily, recording the time of day that the light was turned on and extinguished along with any other activity such as the operation of the fog signal.

After the light was automated, it was placed on a steel tower in the middle of the island until the trees grew too tall and blocked the view. The light was then moved back and attached to the original tower.

Leaving Poverty Island, we proceeded to St. Martin Island where we went ashore to view the lighthouse and explore the island. The buildings there, while vacant, were in fairly good condition. From the abandoned boat dock, the rails of a tram remain. The tram was used to haul supplies from the dock to the keepers dwellings. Two things that linger most in our memories were the profusion of wild flowers in bloom and the many snakes that we found everywhere. We ended our tour with dinner at Washington Island, Wisconsin before boating back to Fairport.

1. - Menominee North Pier Light, 2. - Looking straight up the stairway and circular interior of Peninsula Point tower, exterior is square brick, 3. - Peninsula Point tower, 4. - Lens and top of tower, Sand Point Lighthouse, 5. - Sand Point Lighthouse at Escanaba has had a fascinating history, 6. - Escanaba Harbor Light, 7. - Sand Point, Escanaba, a museum open to the public.

34

2

5

6

7

At Peninsula Point Lighthouse only the yellow brick tower remains, but it is open to the public. Climbing the circular stairs, the view of Lake Michigan and Big and Little Bay De Noc was impressive. To the south was Minneapolis Shoal Light and west several miles was Escanaba's Sand Point Light. Escanaba seemed so close, yet driving there is almost thirty miles by highway.

Later that day, I stood on the tower of Sand Point Lighthouse looking back towards Peninsula Point. Thoughts went through my mind of how the early captains managed these waters before the lights were built, and how many lives have been saved since. And of the lighthouse keepers who took such pride in their duties and yet, in most cases, never met or even saw the sailors who depended on them.

The passengers for Isle Royale were ready to board the first flight on the small seaplane when I arrived. Since all the regular spaces were taken, the only seat available for me was the co-pilot seat. The dependable plane had seen its share of travel as everything seemed well worn. Seats were simply two benches along each side where passengers would face each other during the flight. Traveling along was a happy group of Boy Scouts, with all their camping gear stuffed in, headed for a delightful excursion to Isle Royale National Park.

The twin engine craft with pontoon floats taxied down the Houghton-Hancock waterfront and under the Vertical Lift Bridge before making its long run down the waterway and lifting into the air. Isle Royale was an hour away.

Landing at Rock Harbor, I walked to the marina and rented a small boat with an outboard motor. Isle Royale was such a pretty place, it was difficult to know what to explore first. I had plenty of film, but was short on time

as I had to catch the 4:00 P.M. flight back to Houghton. Everything looked so clean, even the plants seemed to be freshly washed. Going along the shore, the rocks were covered with bright orange lichens which contrasted with the deep blue color of Lake Superior.

After several miles of travel along the shore, the old Rock Harbor Lighthouse came into view. Beaching the boat in a small cove, I went ashore to get different camera viewpoints and to just sit on a rock and contemplate the scene. It was so quiet there. The faintest whisper of the breeze in the trees and a few waves splashing on the rocks provided music. There was not another person anywhere near and even thoughts of highways and cities felt out of place.

All too soon, it was time to return to reality. I really did not want to miss the flight back. Again, I had the honor of riding co-pilot on the return trip to Houghton.

1. - Ontonagon Light,
2. - Sky Ranger seaplane,
3. - Rock Harbor Lighthouse on Isle Royale,
4. - Sand Hills Light,
5. - Eagle Harbor,
6. - Eagle Harbor Lighthouse,
7. - Evening at Eagle Harbor.

5

6

7

Eagle Harbor is a classic lighthouse perched on the rocks of the Keweenaw Peninsula. It displays an alternating red and white beacon signal to mark the harbor. Once there, boaters must pay close attention to the range lights and day markers to navigate a safe course between the rocks that extend almost across the entrance. There is an excellent museum and a viewing platform for visitors to the Eagle Harbor Lighthouse.

Manitou Island

1

2

3

4

5

Leaving the shelter of Copper Harbor and heading into the vast expanse of Lake Superior makes you feel very small and insignificant. There are no smooth beaches here. The rocks slope right down to the water's edge and continue downward below the surface. Just offshore, the depth gage registers water of 300 feet deep. Traveling east, the tip of Keweenaw fades away and in the distance, Manitou Island comes into view. In between, it looks like what appears to be a lighthouse simply sitting on the water. It is Gull Rock. Aptly named, it is home to hundreds of gulls and loons. On approach, the instruments indicate 20 foot boulders beneath me so I proceed with great caution. The water is so clear, I can see the huge rocks all around. The sunlight is best on the opposite side, so I ease in from the other direction. Lake Superior is on good behavior today and the sky is also kind, giving me excellent cloud formations. Today, this rocky outpost will make great photos for sure. Going on to Manitou Island, the clouds remain very pretty. Very often as the day warms, those showy cumulus clouds will evaporate, leaving a solid blue sky. At the island, deep water on one side of the light allows me to bring the boat in very close, but that is not the best angle. The rocks here are unpredictable, and consist of long rows of boulders that angle down into the lake. Between the rocks is a small pebble beach where I was able to secure the boat and go ashore. Cash, my Black Lab dog just jumped over and swam in.

1. - Lake Superior's Manitou Island, 2. - Solar power cells at Manitou, 3. -The author's boat at Manitou Island, 4. - Manitou Lighthouse, 5. - Gull Rock Lighthouse from a seagull's perspective, 6. - Gull Rock

40

6 ➤

1. - Copper Harbor Lighthouse aerial view, 2. - Copper Harbor Lighthouse keepers quarters, 3. - Picturesque Copper Harbor Light, 4. - Panorama view Copper Harbor, 5. - Lighthouse Tour boat, Copper Harbor, 6. - Bete Grise view at Lac La Belle, 7. - Bete Grise Lighthouse, 8. - Keweenaw Waterway Upper Entrance Light.

1

2

3

The lighthouse is automated and gathers power from a large bank of solar cells. The steel tower supporting the light is identical to the one at Whitefish Point. It is an enchanting place with brightly colored lichens covering some of the rocks. Looking in every direction the picture possibilities seem endless. I marvel at the wide range of flowers all in bloom at once. From springtime lilacs, still fragrant, planted long ago by some lighthouse keeper, to the many wild flowers including autumn season goldenrod. Wild strawberries, red raspberries and blueberries all are ripe at the same time, too. Cash is exploring everything with great enthusiasm, and I wonder what his keen sense of smell is telling him.

4

5

6

7

8

Returning to Copper Harbor, the afternoon sunshine glares across the water making it impossible to see the rocks at the harbor entrance. It is then that you appreciate the range lights and day markers that allow you to align one in front of the other and come straight in safely between the rocks!

1. - Portage River (Jacobsville)
Light, 2. - Portage Lake Lower
Entrance Light, 3. - Marquette
panorama, 4. - Presque Isle
Harbor Breakwater Light at
Marquette,
5. - The Charles E. Wilson ore
carrier loading at Marquette's
Presque Isle Harbor Dock,
6. - Marquette Harbor Light,
7. - Big Bay Point Light.

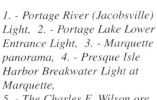

1

2

3

Big Bay Lighthouse is a bed and breakfast, located at the village of Big Bay, twenty-six miles north of Marquette. Having called ahead to request permission to take photographs, I arrived there at the first light of day. The lighthouse sits on a high bluff with a suburb view of Lake Superior. The light of the morning sun was perfect illumination for this red brick structure. Using both 35mm and medium format cameras, the buildings were photographed from all angles possible and the equipment was put away when the keeper of the bed and breakfast invited me in to join his guests for breakfast. He was an excellent cook and very knowledgeable about the area, making the visit a pure delight.

Just as I was leaving, dark storm clouds moved in rapidly from the west. The sun was still shining and a lovely rainbow developed. Making a dash for my equipment and working quickly as possible with cameras on tripods, I took 30 more pictures with the rainbow arching over the stately landmark before the first raindrop hit me. It was the last pictures of the day as it continued to rain until evening.

4

5

6

7

Big Bay Lighthouse

1 ≺

1. - Old Grand Island East Channel
Light, 2. - Grand Island Harbor Rear
Range Light at the village of Christmas,
3. - Grand Island North Light sits high
on a cliff at Grand Island,
4. - Munising Front Range Light,
5. - Pictured Rocks and cruise boat.

2

3

4

5

For anyone visiting lighthouses or exploring Michigan's Upper Peninsula, a Pictured Rocks cruise should be high on the list of things to do. From the cruise, you will have a chance to see the remarkable Pictured Rocks formations and will also get a close-up view of the East Grand Island Light. As part of the cruise, the captains come in close to the lighthouse and allow time to take photos and give interesting information.

The Grand Island East Channel Light, was built in 1868 to mark the Munising harbor entrance. After the Munising Range Lights were built, it ceased operation in 1913. Still standing, it looks lonely and deserted. It is weathered and old with every trace of paint gone.

1. - Keepers quarters at Au Sable Point, 2. - Lake Superior's Shipwreck Coast, 3. - Grand Marais Outer Range Light, 4. - Inner Range Light, 5. - Au Sable Light Station, Grand Marais, 6. - Crisp's Point, 7. - Au Sable Lighthouse in autumn, 8. - Lake Superior.

1

Hurricane River in the Pictured Rocks National Lakeshore area tumbles over a few rocks and dashes across the beach into Lake Superior. There is a small park here and from the campsites you can hear the sounds of water all night long. In the cool of an autumn morning, Cash and I headed off down the mile and a half foot trail to the Au Sable Point Lighthouse. As the trail went along the lake, the weathered remains of a ship, that long ago had washed ashore, could be seen. Ten ships ran aground or were lost along this point. Further along in the damp soil of the path to the lighthouse, we came across very fresh tracks of a black bear, also heading toward the lighthouse. There were lots of wild blueberries, so we may have interrupted the bear's breakfast. Whenever possible, I enjoy walking barefoot and was walking without shoes on this morning. I have often wondered what the next person who came along must have thought, seeing bare footprints, black bear tracks and dog tracks, or if they would even notice.

7

2

3

4

5

6

The keeper's dwelling had extensive restoration since a previous visit, and it is wonderful to see the loving care given to Michigan's historic landmarks. The buildings are empty and silent, but standing there made me wonder about the people who had lived there. Were they lonely? Were they happy in this remote place? Today, one can only imagine.

8

1

2

3

4

W hitefish Point is Michigan's most famous light station. First estab-
lished in 1849, the present structure dates from 1861. While doing
photographs of the lighthouse and restored keepers quarters for a
recently published book, I spent about four days at the lighthouse. Much of
the photography was inside, but while there, the weather gave me almost
everything but snow. It was an interesting variety of conditions.

Much of the restoration of the keepers quarters is in the 1920's era when,
as a child, Bertha Endress lived at the lighthouse while her grandfather was
the lighthouse keeper. Bertha recalls skating with wooden wheel roller skates
on the sidewalks between the buildings since at that time there were no roads
to Whitefish Point and everything came by boat. To illustrate the story, I used
a pair of wooden wheeled roller skates from the museum. Placing them on a
section of the narrow original sidewalk, and with the camera only inches
above, it was possible to get the skates and lighthouse both in one picture.
Using two cameras, the scene was photographed with black and white film
as well as color. An antique brown tone version is shown here. The color
image was used in the Whitefish Point book.

At Whitefish Point as at other light stations, everything was kept neat and
orderly. In spite of the remoteness of the locations, the U.S. Lighthouse
Service made every effort to provide the best living conditions possible for
the light keepers and their families. Visitors enjoy seeing the interiors very
much as they were before the light was automated. The crafts-
manship is outstanding in the construction and woodwork
throughout the facility.

5

6

7

8

1. - Illustration depicting the 1920's story of Bertha Endress
2. - Kitchen cook stove
3. - Sculpture and office of Mr. Carlson, Light keeper
4. - Stairway to second floor and access to lantern room
5. - Dining room
6. - Bedroom
7. - Carlson's Bible
8. - Original Fresnel Lens
9. - Living room
10. - Aero beacon lamps currently in use

10

9

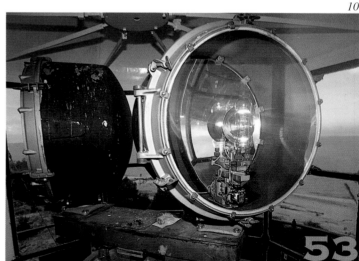

Sunrise, Whitefish Point

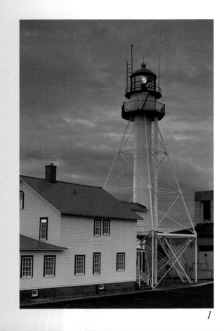

1

2

3

To do well at scenic photography, being adaptable to nature's conditions is important. Even then, there are times when you need a little luck and a lot of patience.

Always experimenting with new ideas, I wondered if it would be possible to light the entire complex with flash at twilight. It would make the buildings lighter than the evening sky and even might look dramatic. Several high power flash units that were used for the museum interiors were used. To power the flash outside, the generator from my motorhome worked just fine. So, in the parking lot after hours, waiting for evening it looked like a movie set. Well, the idea was good, but suddenly there was a big crash! The wind had blown over one of the flash units and it smashed to the pavement. The flash cord was connected to the camera, and that too fell over. Hate it when that happens! Luck was on my side that night as the rubber handles of the tripod took the shock of falling and the camera never touched the ground. The big flash unit had a dent in the reflector and a broken quartz light, but the flash still worked perfectly. The pictures were unique and one was used in a double-spread for a book, another is shown here.

Early one morning when the sun came up, the white building took on a lovely pink color. As the bright sky reflected in the windows, it gave the appearance of lights on within the house. That picture became a calendar cover.

Traveling between the Whitefish Point and Tahquamenon region of Western Chippewa County in the Hiawatha National Forest and the city of Sault Ste. Marie, the most scenic route follows near the shoreline of Whitefish Bay through Brimley. Point Iroquois Lighthouse is near the village of Bay Mills. The lighthouse is open to the public and visitors may climb to the top of the tower for a panoramic view.

1. - Whitefish Point at evening, 2. - Architectural patterns, 3. - Lighthouse flash photograph, 4. - Rotating Second Order Fresnel Lens from White Shoal Lighthouse is on display at Shipwreck Museum, Whitefish Point, 5. - Restored Historic Whitefish Point Light Station, 6. - Iroquois Point Light Station, 7. - Autumn scene at Iroquois Point.

4

5

6

7

Over the years, searching for the perfect spot for a photograph has led me to some unique and interesting places. Sitting on a steel ball with my legs wrapped around a cable, I've been hoisted 200 feet above a construction site. Recently, when an airplane was not available, I went aloft, carrying two cameras around my neck, strapped to a parasail being towed by a boat. It had 800 feet of tether rope, so it was possible to get the "aerials" without an airplane.. Besides, it was great fun. The only problem was that I had to curl my toes to keep my shoes from falling off.

On Round Island, as the restoration of the lighthouse was being completed, the best view of the lighthouse was blocked by a construction crane. I made it work to my advantage by climbing on the boom to get an excellent picture of the lighthouse with the Grand Hotel on Mackinac Island in the background.

On Drummond Island, the pilot who would take me up, had to pump the water out of the pontoons of his vintage 1932 airplane before we could take off. He did enjoy flying low, giving me a good close-up of the lighthouse at DeTour Point. We would cruise at 12 feet above the water, then gain enough altitude to cross over an island. In fact, when he turned for his final approach to set down for the landing, he had to climb high enough so the wing tip would not drag the water.

5

3

6

7

8

1. - Aerial view of Round Island, 2. - Round Island
before restoration, 3. - Round Island Lighthouse,
4. - Panorama of Straits of Mackinac, 5. - Channel
marker at Mackinac Island Harbor, 6. - De Tour
Point Light 7. - De Tour Point Light with freighter
downbound in Lake Huron, 8. - Bois Blanc Lighthouse.

Cheboygan Range Light (center)

1. - Fourteen Foot Shoal Light, 2. - Poe Reef Light, 3. - U.S. Coast Guard Cutter Mackinaw, 4. - Forty Mile Point Lighthouse, 5. - Cheboygan Crib Light, re-located to the breakwater at Cheboygan harbor entrance.

1

2

3

At the Cheboygan boat ramp, the boat slid easily off the trailer and settled in the water. You go through the familiar routine, park the trailer, gather up the things to take, get in the boat and start the engine. This time, there was this "clunk" sound, the kind of noise one really doesn't want to hear. The batteries were down and the starter wouldn't move. But, better to have it happen at the dock than out on the lake. How could I be so dumb as to have left the light on in the cabin? Using jumper cables, the motor was promptly started. Still, it was a good idea to let it charge for a few minutes before heading out. Just then, a summer shower came over and did its share to maintain the lake level. Soon it passed and I went out in northern Lake Huron to photograph Fourteen Foot Shoal Light and Poe Reef Light. The gray sky of the receding storm behind the lighthouses only made the pictures more interesting.

4^   5>

*1. - New (1870) Presque Isle Lighthouse,
2. - Presque Isle Lighthouse at dawn,
3. - Presque Isle's Third Order Fresnel lens
showing back-up lamp detail, 4. - Keepers
residence at Presque Isle, 5. - Old Presque
Isle Light 1840-1870, 6. - Close-up of New
Presque Isle Light.*

3

4

5

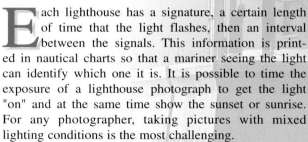

2

6

Each lighthouse has a signature, a certain length of time that the light flashes, then an interval between the signals. This information is printed in nautical charts so that a mariner seeing the light can identify which one it is. It is possible to time the exposure of a lighthouse photograph to get the light "on" and at the same time show the sunset or sunrise. For any photographer, taking pictures with mixed lighting conditions is the most challenging.

I spent the night at Presque Isle Light and was up as the faintest sign of morning began to show in the sky. The glow of dawn made the tower a soft, warm delightful color. I calculated that in order to get the colors of the sky, the total exposure time should be 12 to 16 seconds. The problem was, the signal light was on too long and was too bright to retain the mood of the soft lighting. By covering the lens as the signal light flashed, I was able to get the right balance of light and sky and the pictures came out beautifully. Those pictures have since been used on book covers, calendars and a lighthouse video cover.

Old Presque Isle Light

Sturgeon Point Light

1. - Sturgeon Point Lighthouse and fishing boat, 2. - Sturgeon Point Lighthouse, 3. - Tawas Point Light Station, 4. - Evening at Tawas Point, 5. - Tawas Point Light Station.

1

2

3

While visiting Sturgeon Point Lighthouse, I had parked the motorhome and boat along the road. The combined length is sixty feet and it can easily plug up a parking lot designed for autos, so parking along the road was the best place. In fact, it was the only place. When leaving and backing the trailer around, something in the rear view mirror caught my eye. It seemed the tread from one tire had peeled off, and in doing so had flapped up and smashed the trailer's tail light. The spare tire was in the boat. Dropping the spare over the side, it bounced sideways - right up and smashed the other tail light! Oh well, some days are like that.

Another time visiting Sturgeon Point, with my camera on a tripod, I was out on the spit of land that juts out into Lake Huron. It was early morning, when five deer came out of the woods to drink from the lake. Any motion would alert them to my presence, so there was no chance to put on a telephoto lens and capture the scene. Moving only my eyes, it was fun to watch them drink their fill and wander back into the woods.

4∧ 5>

1. - Point Aux Barques overlooking Lake Huron, 2. - Sunrise, Port Sanilac, 3. - Port Sanilac Lighthouse, 4. - Fort Gratiot Lighthouse, 5. - Aerial, Fort Gratiot at Port Huron, 6. - Lightship Huron's anchor windlass, 7. - Pilot house of Lightship Huron, 8. - Lightship Huron at Port Huron.

Driving to Maine for a three-week assignment to do lighthouse photos for post cards, calendars and books, the shortest route was to go through Canada via Port Huron and on to Niagara Falls. Passing through Port Huron, the morning sky was too beautiful not to stop at the Fort Gratiot Lighthouse. The air was washed clean from overnight showers and the U.S. Coast Guard Light Station was so neat and orderly. The wind made the flags look perfect. Since the sale of stock photographs for publication is part of Penrod/Hiawatha's business, I try to anticipate all the various ways a subject might be used and take many more pictures than one might expect.

In Michigan's lighthouse history, there were several lightships that would be anchored near a hazardous shoal during the shipping season. Some of these lightships were replaced by lighthouses. The 97 foot lightship *Huron* was stationed at Corsica Shoals, about six miles north of the Blue Water Bridge in Southern Lake Huron, for 36 years. Retired from active service in 1971, the *Huron* was the last lightship on the Great Lakes. Volunteers have spent a great deal of time in the restoration of this vessel and in 1989 it was designated a National Historic landmark. It is now open to the public as a museum along the St. Clair River at Port Huron.

4

5

6

7

8

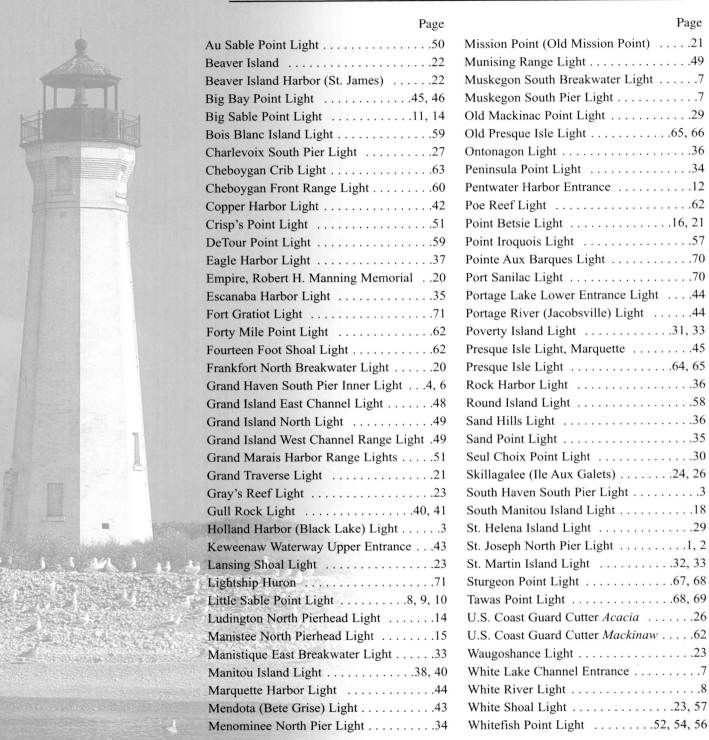

LISTING OF LIGHTHOUSES PICTURED

Not every lighthouse in Michigan is pictured in this selection of photographs. The map on the following page will be helpful to visually realize just how many lighthouses Michigan has and to see their approximate locations.